Robert Jemison, Jr.
A Man With Vision

Elbert S. Jemison, Jr.
Wendell O. Givens

Seacoast Publishing

Library of Congress Control Number: 2005937158

ISBN 1-59421-018-7

Printed in the United States of America

To obtain copies of this book, visit local bookstores and gift shops. For information about using this book for fundraising purposes or corporate gifts contact:

Seacoast Publishing, Inc.
Post Office 26492
Birmingham, Alabama 35260
seacoast@charter.net

Contents

Why This Book

"I believe it's a tragedy if you don't leave the world what you know." —*Golfer Gary Player*

Speakers and writers without number have quoted this question-and-answer:

"But why did you climb the mountain?"

"Because it was there."

Why do I write a book about Robert Jemison, Jr., my Uncle Bob? Because his remarkable life is there, has been there for decades, needing an author.

Why should a family member write the account of Robert Jemison, Jr.'s life when seasoned writers, some of whom knew him well, abound?

Logical question. One presumed answer: Because Robert Jemison, Jr., is still too recent, too familiar, some may say; accomplishments will come into sharper focus.

Perhaps so. But several factors persuaded me to act now. As one of his staunchest admirers, I recall my uncle-nephew relationship with him as an inspiration and joy, although I confess that in my early years I didn't really understand or appreciate his greatness.

I had long known of the many accolades bestowed on Uncle Bob and of the extensive information available about him in libraries and in family files and scrapbooks.

Therefore, it seemed to me that it was time to compile and consolidate the information about his incredible life into book form.

We hope that family members, friends, librarians, historians and residents of the many areas he developed will welcome *Robert Jemison, Jr.: A Man With Vision.*

--Elbert S. Jemison, Jr.

Dedication

To family members and friends who encouraged us to produce this account of Robert Jemison, Jr.'s remarkable life. Many of them provided vital information and photographs.

With Thanks

The authors wish to thank (in no special order) the many persons and organizations who helped make possible this book on Robert Jemison, Jr.

They include Louise G. "Weesie" Smith, Caroline M. Jemison, Anne Jemison and Rest B. Heppenstall, Marvin Whiting, A.H. "Rick" Woodward, III, Carol Jemison and Alex S. Lacy, Thomas M. West, Jr., Phil Dorn, Jr., John C. Stapleton, Philip Jackson, Jr., Nita Moorehead, University of the South archivist Anne Armour, Thomas N. Carruthers, Mary Caroline G. Boothby, Elberta G. Reid, Cathy Adams, Dave Mace. C.H "Hop" Chichester, Jr., Richard Grooms, Olene Parker, Sam S. Gaston, Henry Lynn, Jr., Doug Shook, Betsy Turner Allison, Bill Harrison, Elizabeth Wells, Tom Self, Benny Yates, John W. Jemison of Kingwood, Texas, Jess Ann Jemison, Mary Anne Givens, Janis L. Bailey, Marjorie L. White, Craig Allen, Jr., staff members in the Birmingham Public Library's Southern History, Social Sciences and Archives departments and *The Birmingham News, Birmingham Post-Herald* and *Birmingham Magazine.*

Robert Jemison, Jr.'s creed

This excerpt from an 1825 Daniel Webster anniversary speech at the Bunker Hill Battle site became Uncle Bob's lifetime creed.

"Let us develop the resources of our land, call forth its powers, build up the institutions, promote all its great interests, and see whether we also, in our day and generation, may not perform something worthy to be remembered."

I.
The Man and His Creed

Let's ask an intriguing question up front.

What if Robert Jemison, Jr., had not come this way? What if his parents, instead of riding their covered wagon from Tuscaloosa to Birmingham in 1884, had gone northwest to Memphis or perhaps on to Oklahoma?

Numerous questions would cry out for answers.

Without Robert Jemison, Jr., would Fairfield, U.S. Steel Corp.'s model mill town, have been as well planned?

Would such communities as Central Park, Forest Park, Redmont and Mountain Brook have even been developed? Would the Country Club of Birmingham and Mountain Brook Club golf courses have been designed by world-famous course architect Donald Ross, and have won applause from local and national golfers?

Would landmark Birmingham structures such as the Tutwiler Hotel, Ridgely Apartments, Empire Building and numerous others have been built?

Would some other Birmingham man have been hailed as "Realtor of the Century" and another as "the South's Man of the Year"?

Perhaps I should condense all the what-ifs to this: How different would Birmingham be today had Robert Jemison, Jr. not come this way?

As an admittedly admiring nephew, I will put him on record as thoroughly and accurately as I can.

The scope of his remarkable life and accomplishments filled me with awe and pride as I put this account together. Despite having seen firsthand much of his work and despite my vantage point as nephew, I wondered how any person could undertake and successfully complete all that he did.

From his seemingly humble beginning, arriving in Birmingham with his family in a covered wagon, he proceeded in adulthood to being acclaimed "Realtor of the Century" and "the person who put the magic in the Magic City."

I pondered for many hours how best to introduce you to Robert Jemison, Jr. He was Uncle Bob to me and to all nieces and nephews. To close friends he was Bob. To others, perhaps not as close, he was Mr. Bob, and was approached with a sense of admiration and respect.

Noted newspaper columnist John Temple Graves wrote in

Dixie Business *magazine's spring 1972 cover proclaimed Uncle Bob "Man of the South for 1971." (Courtesy University of Georgia Business Library)*

1959 that Uncle Bob "is entitled to be called Birmingham's most founding father." He added that "the best of Birmingham might not have been born if Robert Jemison, Jr., had not been born."

In Uncle Bob's early business years he chose as his creed the words from Early American orator Daniel Webster's inspired anniversary address at the site of the Battle of Bunker Hill. Thus, Webster helped to inspire him to "perform something worthy to be remembered." The words personify Robert Jemison, Jr.

After Uncle Bob planned and helped give birth to suburban Fairfield, U.S. Steel's model mill town, former President Theodore Roosevelt called him "a corker," applauding him for his work developing Fairfield.

Despite that and other accolades, I know my beloved uncle as one of the warmest, most down-to-earth human beings on the planet. Guided by the Webster creed, from his youth to the end of his life he focused on serving his fellow man, on helping to make the world a better place for all to live.

Despite his impressive success in business, I never felt Uncle Bob's principal purpose in life was to make money. I saw him always as striving to make life better for others--in their homes, their environment, their day-to-day lives.

He would have been successful in any other chosen career. He personified confidence, inspiration and leadership, and he was always the perfect gentleman. He was caring, respectful and polite to everyone in all walks of life.

In development of Mountain Brook, he stretched his finances almost to the breaking point, so much so that associates urged him to use bankruptcy for relief. His financial problems were caused by the depression that began in 1929. But he was adamant against taking that way out. He vowed to cover every dollar of debt, and he did.

Early on, he delighted in attending Jemison family gatherings such as Sunday dinners at his parents' Glen Iris residence. And late in life when he had become a gentleman farmer at his Spring Lake Farms northeast of Birmingham, he invited family members to visit him, Aunt Virginia and their children. As related further on, I occasionally bicycled there with buddies for weekend fun.

Also as noted later, Uncle Bob helped cement the family by keeping close check on family members, writing and phoning often to encourage us. He wrote me when I was attending Sewanee Military Academy, when I competed in golf tournaments and especially after I entered World War Two combat. This chapter is intended as a kind of introduction to what follows: a detailed account of Robert Jemison, Jr.'s life, inspired by Daniel Webster's creed.

II.
Meeting the Family

Occasionally I'm asked how I am related to Robert Jemison, Jr. As son of Elbert Jemison, one of Uncle Bob's four brothers, I am a nephew. And if you read that as a lead-in to Uncle Bob's family tree, you're right.

Until I began work on this book, I was never really excited about genealogy, but I accepted a suggestion to check on our Jemison tree.

Two source books differed about where the first Jemison (in our clan) to live in America came over from; one said Scotland; the second, Ireland. They did agree that he (Robert, first of many Roberts) in 1730 chose Pennsylvania as his new home and there with his wife reared seven sons.

One of those seven, another Robert, eventually moved to Georgia's Lincoln County and fought in the American Revolution. The family line descended through William Henry Jemison, born in Tuscaloosa, Ala., Sept. 12, 1853, and father of Robert Jemison, Sr., who in 1884 moved to bustling new Birmingham.

Through published reports and family information relayed to

The Robert Jemison Sr. family's first Birmingham home, downtown on North 20th Street. From here young Bob attended Powell School. (Courtesy, Birmingham Public Library Archives)

me, I became familiar with the impressive role my grandfather Robert Jemison, Sr., had played in early Birmingham. Surprising to me, he at first had not planned to make Birmingham his new home; Los Angeles had been his goal. But he became attracted to Birmingham's bustling young businesses and saw opportunities. So, he stayed.

Grandfather Jemison had been in the hardware business in Tuscaloosa and resumed in that business in Birmingham. He also grew interested in real estate development because he foresaw the area's potential for growth.

15

Robert Jemison, Sr. on the cover of Jemison Realty Co. magazine, placed there by son Robert Jr. to honor him.

According to *The Birmingham News*, in later years Grandfather "proved himself a masterful executive by consolidating nine competing streetcar lines, three electric light companies, and a gas company into the Birmingham Railway, Light and Power Co."

In 1898, *The News* reported, Robert Jemison, Sr., formed City Land Co. and bought 40 acres on the northern slope of Red Mountain, brought in a leading landscape architect to design a homeplace for him "and a few congenial friends" and named the area Glen Iris Park.

Uncle Bob had been born in Tuscaloosa Feb. 28, 1878, one of seven children born to Grandfather and Eugenia Sorsby Jemison.

The Glen Iris home of Uncle Bob's parents.

At some point many years later (perhaps a newspaper or family member had requested it), Uncle Bob decided to produce a family data sheet. What follows is precisely the way he worded it, listing his father's grandparents, parents and children.

The "Rambling Reminiscences" part of the "title" makes me think perhaps Uncle Bob had planned to write a lot more but didn't get around to it. Or, a more intriguing possibility--he did reminisce more and left some fascinating Jemison stories, as yet unfound but possibly hidden away among family keepsakes!

This Glen Iris community marker reads: Founded in 1898 by Robert Jemison, this 30-acre historic district is a private residential park containing an almost intact collection of some of Birmingham's finest 20th century houses. It was the first professionally landscaped community in the city and the first where residents adhered to strictly self-imposed rules and covenants. The marker was placed in August 1981 by the National Register of Historic Places.

THE JEMISON COMPANIES
BIRMINGHAM, ALABAMA

August 7, 1950.

Mrs. A. H. Woodward,
Mrs. L. C. Morris,
Mr. John S. Jemison,
Mr. Sorsby Jemison,
Mr. Elbert S. Jemison.

My dear Sisters and Brothers:

For your information the sale of the Glen Iris home has been completed. All personal property has been distributed and removed, and the place has been delivered to the new owner, Mr. E. C. Sloss.

I know you share with me a feeling of deep sentiment and personal regret that it seemed wise to let this one, that we all loved and enjoyed for fifty years, pass out of the hands of the family; a home that meant so much to our beloved parents, and in which we have, over a period of fifty years, been together on many occasions of joy and, naturally, some of sorrow.

As I am satisfied that it was not possible or consistent for my family, or any other members of our immediate families, to continue to occupy this home, I realize that it was the wise and proper procedure to sell this place which has meant so much in the past fifty years to all of us. While we no longer have the privilege of assembling as a happy family with our parents in this home at Glen Iris, I believe all of us have the desire to carry on as best we can, and in accordance with the ideals and traditions of our parents, and live up to our heritage as best we can.

In this connection, I feel that you and your children may be interested in again having a copy of that beautiful letter written by Father on June 24, 1926, before leaving for his summer vacation in Massachusetts, where he became ill. In my opinion, we cannot read too often this very beautiful letter.

May I also take this occasion to thank each and every one of you for your cooperation with me in my efforts to carry on and conserve our interests following the depression of the early 30's. May God bless all of you and give you health, happiness and guidance in the way that will make us all worthy of our heritage.

Affectionately,

Bob

RJjr:cc
encl:

Uncle Bob wrote this letter to family members concerning the sale of the Glen Iris family home in 1950.

June 24, 1926.

To My Beloved Wife and Dear Children:

At my death, I would like to be dressed in a suit which I am used to wearing, and as soon as practicable my body to be placed in a coffin and the coffin closed; and I wish a plain, neat, inexpensive coffin.

I hope my daughters will not put on mourning garments for me, Personally, I would prefer my wife did not do so, but would defer to usage and public opinion and would not embarrass them.

I urge upon each one the supreme importance of the Christian Life as the best for this world, as well as for the world to come, and I beg that each one will become a part of the active life of the church, believing that in this way one may best increase his own moral development and also be the means of aiding in every way his fellow man, and I would emphasize the vital importance of simple faith in Christ, love for mankind, a kindly heart, kindly words and helpful deeds.

In having their mother as friend and counsellor I consider my children highly favored. In addition to a mother's love, she is furnished with a wonderful capacity for managing affairs, and I have absolute confidence that she will act and advise for the best interests of her children, and I request that great deference shall be had for her judgment and wishes.

I urge upon my children to make their best friends of each other, and keep presented an unbroken friendly family, in close heart touch for mutual helpfulness, and to this end the stronger must bear with the weaker with patience and in love, and never forsake any one who shall fall in wrong ways, but stick to him or her, and stay by such an one and save such an one, and from such as this sad experience may God in His Wisdom and mercy save my family when I am gone!

I charge all in business to stand together and help each other and be patient and try to cultivate the habit of seeing and hearing the best in each other, and in all mankind. In conduct there is but one rule that is safe and that will do to live by: DO RIGHT.

I hope each one will form the habit of thinking about and trying to cheer and help the young, the unfortunate, the helpless and the sinning whom they meet in life, and try not to spend upon themselves money unnecessarily. That part of my life which I now consider of the most satisfaction consists in the few kind words which I may have done to the humble ones of earth, and the best of these are those in which I have given myself in sympathy and in service, and not any little money gifts.

Do not live for self entirely. Take an interest in and be a part of movements of a public character, intended to help mankind. Go with the good people who are trying to do good. I have never lived up to my standards, and I rely upon the mercy of God through Jesus Christ.

Affectionately,

Robert Jemison.

Robert Jemison, Sr.'s letter to his family as he looked ahead to his death.

Jemisons by the numbers:

Eugenia and Robert Jemison, Sr., hosted this 1926 family gathering at their home on Glen Iris Circle. The authors added the numbers for convenient identification. 1. Anne Woodward 2. Lewis Morris 3. Eugenia Woodward 4. Sorsby Jemison 5. Joe Woodward 6. Martee Woodward 7. Bessie Jemison Morris 8. A.H. "Rick" Woodward 9. Annie Jemison Woodward 10. A.H. "Al" Woodward, Jr. 11. Bob Goodall 12. Bill Jemison 13. Robert Jemison, Sr. 14 Ed Morris 15. Eugenia Sorsby Jemison 16. Bob Jemison, III 17. Virginia Jemison Goodall with (unnumbered) infant Virginia "Din" Goodall 18. house butler William Page 19. John Jemison, Jr. 20. Virginia Walker Jemison 21. Robert Jemison, Jr. 22. Margaret P. Jemison 23. John Jemison 24. Elizabeth Morris 25. Dean Dillard Jemison 26. Helen Jemison 27. Elbert Jemison 28. Elbert Jemison, Jr. 29. Leonard Jemison. (Courtesy, Jemison family collection)

20

Rambling Reminiscences and
Miscellaneous Family Data.

By ROBT. JEMISON JR.

Re: ROBERT JEMISON - 1853-1926

Grand-Parents
Nicholas Turner Sorsby
Born in North Carolina in 1818
Died in Eutaw, Ala. Feb. 27, 1868
Ann Eliza Hill Sorsby,
Born in Greene Co., Ala., March 28, 1837
Died in Birmingham, Ala., Sept. 12, 1920.

William Henry Jemison,
Born in Georgia on March 4, 1820.
Died in East Lake, Ala., Nov. 11, 1892.

Elizabeth Ann Patrick Jemison
Born in Tenn. - Jan. 8, 1821
Died in Tuscaloosa, Ala., June 17, 1891.

Parents:
Robert Jemison
and
Eugenia Rebecca Sorsby.
Married in Christ's Church
in Tuscaloosa, Ala.
October 25, 1876.

Rev. Geo. H. Hunt, D.D., officiating.

Children
Robert Jemison, Jr.
John Snow Jemison
Annie Hill Jemison
Elizabeth Patrick Jemison
Sorsby Jemison
Elbert Sevier Jemison
Richard Wilmer Jemison

I think it's appropriate to continue Uncle Bob's branch of the Jemison family tree, listing his children, grandchildren, and great grandchildren.

Children
Robert Jemison, III
William W. Jemison
Virginia Jemison Goodall

Grandchildren
Carol Jemison Lacy
Ann Jemison Epps
Virginia (Din) Goodall Johnson
Louise (Weesie) Goodall Smith
Eugenia (Genie) Goodall Brannan
William W. Jemison, Jr.
Mary Jemison Grover

Great Grandchildren

Mary Stuart Johnson Young (Zachry)
Virginia Walker Johnson Jones (Bill)
Katherine Payne Johnson Nielsen (Claude)
Irene Acree Johnson Botsford (Kenneth)

Robert Montgomery Goodall Smith (Susan)
Anne Kidder Smith (Rolando Garcia)
Marshall Hopkinson Smith (Lindsay)
Wilson Kidder Smith
Lindsay Crawford Smith, Jr.

Wade Hampton Brannon, Jr. (Camille)
Virginia Irene Brannon Wilson

John Blakeway Lacy (Elizabeth)
Joan Elizabeth Lacy Chancey
Alexander Shelton Lacy, Jr. (Tabitha)

John Michael Epps (Carolyn)
Robert Burton Epps (Michelle)
Stephen Jemison Epps (Donna)
Bruce Blakeway Epps (Amy)
Elizabeth Ann Epps Bowers (Thomas)

Mary Jemison Grover Miller (Dwight)
Elizabeth Stallings Grover Guffey (Steve)
John Calvin Stallings Grover (Beth)
Madeleine Ruffner Grover DeLong

Virginia Morrow Jemison Jones (Christopher)
Caroline Morrow Jemison Alford (David)
William Walker Jemison III

Uncle Bob had 13 nieces and nephews and was devoted to them all. As of this writing three survive: Anne Woodward Lundbeck, Jeanie Jemison Matthews and Elbert S. Jemison, Jr. All reside in Mountain Brook, Ala.

III.
A Head Start in Education

After inquiring at length into Uncle Bob's education, I felt I should remind readers of a sometimes-overlooked but critical part of it. I call it head start.

No, not the government's pre-school program with which all of us are familiar. I refer to the decided advantage Uncle Bob inherited by being born into a reasonably well-off extended Jemison family, most of whose members were well-educated and leaders in public life.

As I see it, Robert Jemison, Jr., got his head start through beneficial genes. Two brief examples:

Uncle Bob's paternal grandfather, William Henry Jemison, was a Princeton graduate, legislator and college professor. Uncle Bob's father, Robert, Sr., was a University of Alabama graduate and, as already noted, a distinguished leader on the early-Birmingham business scene.

That's why I submit that Uncle Bob began life with head-start genes.

Now a look at his formal schooling.

THE "OLD POWELL SCHOOL."
Birmingham's First School Building. Erected in 1873.

Powell School, Birmingham's first, as it looked when Robert Jemison, Jr. attended. (Courtesy, Birmingham Library Archives).

At age 6 he was enrolled at young Birmingham's downtown Powell School only a few blocks from his parents' home on North 20th Street, at the time the city's only public school.

In 1894, when Robert, Jr., had turned 16, his parents enrolled him in South Highlands Academy, a selective private school on Birmingham's south side at 16th Street South and Avenue K.

In his school catalogue, Principal Joel C. DuBose stated that Academy graduates could, without examination, be admitted to the University of Alabama or to the University of Tennessee. Academy graduation certificates, he said, also would be "valuable passports" to other universities.

In the 1894 academy rollbook Uncle Bob was accompanied

Catalogue of Students.

FOR SESSION 1894–95.

STUDENT.	PARENT OR GUARDIAN
John P. Adams	Mr. Geo. G. Adams
Jas. T. Allen	Mr. Jas. A. Allen
Miss Sue Allen Ball	Maj. Geo. C. Ball
Miss Eula Beasley	Mr. Walter L. Beasley
Mr. Walter L. Beasley	
Brett R. Brown	Mr. W. S. Brown
Owen Brown	Mr. W. S. Brown
Carl Brown	Chas. G. Brown, Esq
Miss Mollie Cullom	Mr. E. N. Cullom
Walter Drennen	Dr. Chas. Drennen
Benj. W. DuBose	Mr. Joel C. DuBose
Miss Alice V. DuBose	Mr. Joel C. DuBose
Miss Martha M. DuBose	Mr. Joel C. DuBose
Paul H. Earle, Jr	Mr. Paul H. Earle, Sr
Maxie Elliott	Mr. C. N. Elliott
Moody Forbes	Mr. G. B. Forbes
Jas. Ryan Garner	Mr. J. H. Garner
Mr. Thos. H. Harris	
John C. Henley, Jr	Maj. John C. Henley Sr
Richard H. Herring	Maj. W. W. Herring
Ira L. Hood	Mr. Wm. Hood
Robert D. Hudson	Mr. Joseph McLester
Mr. Chas. H. Jackson	
Robert Jemison, Jr	Mr. Robert Jemison, Sr
John S. Jemison	Mr. Robert Jemison, Sr
Macon L. Jones	Mrs. W. H. Jones
Miss Daisy Lewis	Ivey F. Lewis, Esq
Mr. Walter S. Lide	
Henry W. Lockwood	Mr. J. L. Lockwood

A portion of South Highlands Academy school roll, including Robert Jr. and brother John. (Courtesy, Birmingham Library Southern History Department).

by his brother John. Among several other familiar Birmingham-area names were two VIPs-to-be: Mortimer Jordan and Herbert Tutwiler.

Class groups were listed as sub-primary, primary, intermediate and academic. Courses included English, French, Latin, Greek, arithmetic, algebra, physics, geography and chemistry.

Robert Jemison, Jr. at about 16 years. (from a family group photo)

However the arrangement came about, in 1895 Uncle Bob entered the University of Alabama as a sophomore, identified as in the class of 1898. Surprising to me, his "course" was listed as mining engineering.

Checking the UA yearbook *Corolla*, we found that he was a member of Alabama Alpha of Phi Theta Delta fraternity and an associate member of the campus YMCA.

In 1897 Uncle Bob transferred to the University of the South at Sewanee, Tenn. Perusing the *Sewanee Purple* campus paper and the *Cap and Gown* yearbook in his day disclosed an apparent budding friendship between Uncle Bob and Montgomery's Henry Goldthwaite "Diddy" Seibels, who captained the 1899 Sewanee "Iron-Men" football team that shut out five major opponents in six days, an incredible sports feat. Seibels and Uncle Bob teamed up as officers in the Alabama

28

Club at Sewanee, Uncle Bob as vice president, Diddy as secretary. Both also began what would become loyal alumni support by, while in school, joining the Sewanee Junior Alumni, an organization whose goal was to keep alumni in touch with one another. The group raised money to improve the university's Hardee Park.

Uncle Bob as a University of the South student. (Courtesy, the Cap and Gown *yearbook)*

Uncle Bob's second and final year at Sewanee was devoted principally to studying law.

His file in Sewanee Archives contains a sheaf of letter copies thanking him for his support of Sewanee. This comment from then-historiographer Arthur Ben Chitty is typical: "Thank you for your personal generosity to Sewanee, for your never-failing thoughtfulness and for the initiative you have shown repeatedly in pushing forward Sewanee's hopes."

Uncle Bob added to his support of the university by serving as trustee and regent. His well-rounded education obviously served him well in the productive career that lay ahead.

IV.

The Wedding

The following account of Miss Virginia Walker's marriage to Robert Jemison, Jr., Nov. 12, 1901, was published next day in the Birmingham Age-Herald. We thought readers would like a full reprint.

ROBT. JEMISON, JR. WEDS
MISS VIRGINIA WALKER

No more representative audience ever gathered in Birmingham than the one that assembled at the Church of the Advent last evening. The immediate occasion was the uniting in holy bonds of matrimony Mr. Robert Jemison, Jr., and Miss Virginia Earle Walker. In their union two of the oldest and most prominent families in the State were united, and two young people who have been universally popular.

The church was filled to its utmost seating capacity long before the wedding hour arrived, and still the people thronged the church until the side aisles and front of the church were crowded with eager guests.

The ushers seated the immense crowd most tactfully and gracefully. Fully one-half the church had been reserved for the immediate friends and guests of the family and even these seats were all filled with ladies and gentlemen in full evening dress some time before the arrival of the wedding party.

Miss Belle McCoy presided at the organ and the waiting guests were entertained most delightfully with sweet strains from the organ. The vast throng had waited patiently for the appointed hour and seemed to enjoy every preliminary feature of the wedding ceremony. The church was beautifully decorated in white and green. Stately palms and ferns filled the chancel and circled round the altar; and magnificent white chrysanthemums were twined in profusion around the altar railing. White satin ribbons which divided the aisle were held in place by great bunches of the same nodding yet graceful flowers.

Finally the sweet peals of the wedding march from Lohengrin announced the arrival of the wedding party and expectancy was the qui vive. The ushers, Messrs. Edwin Warner, Hill Ferguson, Frank Smith, Culpepper Exum, John Jemison and Warner Shook, walked down the center aisles two by two and took up their position on either side of the chancel steps.

Then came the bridesmaids, Misses Annie Jemison, Anna Morrow, Estelle Shook of Nashville, Evelyn Young of Louisville, Daisy Moody, Lucy Hagood, Amy Jordan and Lula Brown. And the groomsmen, who were Messrs. William Mudd Walker, Porter Walker, William Mudd Martin, Erskine Ramsay, Paschal Shook, Henry Snow of Tuscaloosa, T.S. Parrott of Newnan, Ga., and Jemison Prowell. The attendants entered alternately and crossing before the altar took up their positions in a semi-circle. The maid of honor, Miss Louise Walker, entered, followed by the bride on the arm of her father. As they reached the chancel steps the Rev. John G. Murray, followed by the groom and his best man, Mr. Hinds Peevey, entered and joined the bride at the altar. The beautiful Episcopal service was very impressive, and the vast audience stood almost breathless during the ceremony. Then the young couple were pronounced man and wife, and the peals from the sweet organ announced the end of the marriage service.

The bride's dress was a magnificent confection of white pompadour silk, trimmed in deep flounces of rose point lace. She carried an exquisite bouquet of pink orchids and lilies of the valley.

The maid of honor wore point d'esprit over green taffeta and carried white chrysanthemums tied with white satin ribbons. The bridesmaids all wore exquisite white gowns and carried white chrysanthemums tied with green ribbons.

Mrs. Robert Jemison, the mother of the groom, was exceptionally handsome in a toilette of creamed striped satin lace made in the becoming princess effect. Mrs. William A. Walker was attired in an elegant costume of black tulle and lace over white satin.

The audience remained seated until all of the family and reception guests had left the church, and this gave the final touch to a wedding that was in every detail perfect.

The reception which followed the ceremony at the church was held in the home of Mr. and Mrs. William A. Walker, the parents of the bride. The entire house was most elaborately decorated for the happy occasion and presented a truly royal scene during the evening when thronged with the numerous friends who had come to tender greetings and congratulations to the young couple.

Mr. and Mrs. Walker received their guests in the drawing room, assisted by Mr. and Mrs. Robert Jemison, Jr., and all the members of the wedding party. Mr. and Mrs. Robert Jemison, Sr., and others. The drawing room was elaborately decorated with bamboo, and the spacious fireplace and windows were banked with quantities of white chrysanthemums. Over the portal hung the wedding bell arranged most artistically of white chrysanthemums and roses.

The roomy hallway was decorated in bamboo and rich yellow chrysanthemums, while in the library soft Persian tinted flowers blended with the oriental draperies and furnishings of the room. In the dining room the center table was chaste and appropriately decorated in white satin and tulle with tracery of smilax and softly glimmering tapers in rich silver candelabras. Elegant refreshments were served during the entire evening. In the hallway was placed the white wedding cake in the suggestive shape of a heart. Tiny ribbons enabled the youthful guests to draw for the trophies within which suggested the future fortunes of the fortunate winner. In the library was placed a flowing bowl of champagne cup. The wedding presents which were displayed in the upper hallway of the house were handsomer and more numerous than any ever displayed in Birmingham. From the beautiful array it would seem that every friend in town and out of town had sweetly remembered the young couple in this substantial way. Not only was the collection an unusually large one, but each and every piece of silver or china was a rare specimen of art in itself, and the collection of cut glass, which was most elaborate and beautiful, comprised every thing that could possibly be used in the home. The many handsome pieces of solid silver were unusually rare and beautiful. Among the presents also were most exqui-site specimens of bronze, vases, sets of plates in cases, berry sets, pictures, beautiful beyond any possible description of enumeration. If kind words and hearty congratulations have power to win long life, happiness and prosperity, then indeed will the future of Mr. and Mrs. Robert Jemison, Jr., be filled to overflowing with all the good things of life. The young couple left at a late hour on their wedding journey and will not return for some weeks.

*Virginia Earle Walker as Mrs. Robert
Jemison, Jr., presumably photographed
in the early years of her marriage.
(Courtesy, Weesie G. Smith)*

*Episcopal Church of the Advent, scene of the
Walker-Jemison wedding. (Courtesy,
Cathedral Church of the Advent)*

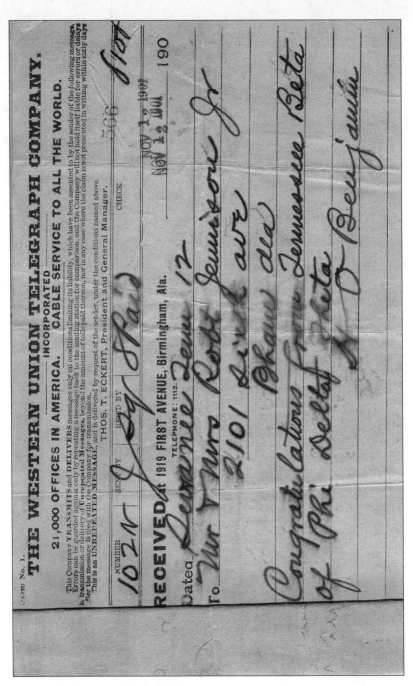

Congratulatory 1901 telegram from Phi Delta Theta, Uncle Bob's fraternity at Sewanee. (Courtesy, Caroline M. Jemison)

V.

Lasting Memories

What follows are samplings of my relationship with Uncle Bob Jemison. Among my intentions: To help assure readers that I knew him sufficiently well to record this account of a remarkable man.

From time to time I'm been asked what type person he was and how we are related. The latter is more easily answered. He and my dad were brothers, so obviously I'm his nephew.

What type of person was Robert Jemison, Jr.? I felt that he was proud to be an American and grateful that he had the opportunity to make his community a better and more attractive place to live.

Having had the privilege of knowing President Gerald R. Ford, I saw Ford similarities to Uncle Bob: Great statesman, honest, caring, always wanting to do right and in a most unpretentious manner.

He was committed all his life to making the world a better place, the type person you'd love to have as a neighbor.

The title of Harry Emerson Fosdick's long-time best-seller

The Power of Positive Thinking fits Uncle Bob to a T. I've never known a more positive thinker or greater optimist, and I think his business associates and other friends would agree. Once more I refer readers to the creed he adapted from orator Daniel Webster. Be familiar with that creed (printed at the start of this text) and you will begin to know Robert Jemison, Jr.

As I have noted, I was one of his staunchest admirers. I knew him as a caring uncle, having visited in his home many times and on uncounted other occasions at his and my father's real estate office.

My treasured uncle-nephew relationship was an inspiration and a joy. But a confession of sorts seems appropriate here. In my younger years I realize now that I neither understood nor appreciated his unwavering commitments and his many accomplishments. But that understanding and recognition would come in full measure later in my life.

My first memory of Uncle Bob was a gathering of the family at my grandparents' home in Glen Iris for a group picture. I am told that the family celebration was the christening of Virginia "Din" Goodall. That was in 1926 and I was 5.

Still very clear in my memory is the 1927 day I accompanied my dad and Uncle Bob to their Jemison-Seibels company office to watch Birmingham's motorcade salute to Charles A. Lindbergh soon after Lindy's solo flight across the Atlantic

Ocean.

After the motorcade swung onto North 21st Street, the three of us stood close to a second-floor window and cheered the heroic American who had won world attention with his courageous flight. I felt privileged to have that close-up view of a genuine hero. And grateful to share it with two persons I admired.

My Jemison grandparents' spacious Glen Iris home until 1950 was the scene of many family Sunday dinners. Remembering those get-togethers, I still get warm feelings knowing how Uncle Bob must have filled with pride on every such occasion because all his life he was family-oriented. He kept close tab on everything we did as a group and as individuals.

He would ask around about what was going on, what we had accomplished and what projects were ahead. He cared and he made that caring known through counseling and encouraging.

If I were asked to choose my favorite boyhood memories of Uncle Bob, that wouldn't be difficult: My summertime bicycle trips to his and Aunt Virginia's Spring Lake Farms in northeast Jefferson County, just beyond the Birmingham border. Those trips are described in detail in another chapter, but must be mentioned here because that memory of Uncle Bob lives delightedly to this day. I hope that remembering our camping-out days at Spring Lake Farms has stayed with early-teen buddies Bob Ramsay, Henry Badham, Van Scott,

May 8, 1945

Dear Elbert,

We are naturally thinking of you today and others near
and dear to us in the Armed Forces and thanking God
that you have been spared up to this important milestone
in the defeat of Germany, and we are also hoping and
praying that it will result in your early return home,
safe and sound, with a clear conscience and satisfaction
of having done your duty in this great crisis.

All of us naturally have a feeling which mingles relief,
joy and delight, along with a solemn, thankful feeling
of gratitude for the outcome with Germany and the hope
that it will hasten the day of victory over Japan.

May God bless you and give you a safe return home very
soon.

All the family join me in love and best wishes on this
eventful day in our world's history.

Very affectionately,
Uncle Bob

Capt. Elbert S. Jemison, 0-443142
28th Reconnaissance Troop
APO 28, c/o Postmaster
New York, N. Y.

*Uncle Bob's letter to me as World War II in Europe ended. His
postscript (in longhand) reads, "We have enjoyed those fine and
interesting letters, and we are relieved that you are relieved of
combat service for a while at least. Hope you will get in the army
of occupation rather than more fighting with the Japs. Best of
luck to you, Ed Sebree (general to whom I had been aide and
served under in combat) and other friends."*

43

and Charley Nice, among others.

When development of Mountain Brook (1927-29) was Uncle Bob's principal project, on Sundays I would ride with him and my dad (real estate associates) for an off-day check on the progress of that development. Did I see a special gleam of pride in their eyes? Years later, I have convinced myself that I did.

In 1934 when I was 13 I rode to Selma with Dad and Uncle Bob to see the antebellum homes there. In addition to the history we saw, I presume the two real estate pros were scouting for homebuilding features that might be attractive in Birmingham.

After graduation from Sewanee Military Academy in 1940, I was in Uncle Bob's office being congratulated for having been appointed cadet lieutenant-colonel and battalion commander, for having been football team captain and at graduation having been presented the academy's Sevier Sabre as SMA's outstanding cadet. Vice Chancellor Alex Guerry had presented the sabre.

In 1942, after I had been commissioned a 2nd lieutenant and ordered to Army duty, I was visiting Uncle Bob in his real estate office. He told me he was proud of my being commissioned and said he knew I would be a fine officer and would continue a family tradition of doing my duty.

I think Uncle Bob would have been delighted to serve in the military, but he was much beyond the eligible age.

While I was in France I was promoted to captain, and of course that pleased him. When the war finally ended while I was in combat in Germany, he wrote me how relieved he was that I had survived a lot of war.

Another favorite memory is driving Uncle Bob to Sewanee in the early 1950s for a meeting of the University of the South Board of Trustees, of which he was a member. He could drive but wasn't fond of it. I was delighted, principally because it gave us hours for small talk on a variety of subjects.

I wanted to hear about his latest land-development projects and his numerous endeavors for his community: the Community Chest and Red Cross fund campaigns, for examples.

In turn, as he always did, he asked me about my latest golf accomplishments and how I was progressing in the insurance business, and about any of my upcoming activities. And because he was so family-oriented, we discussed what was happening in other Jemison families.

Predictably, he was at the Mountain Brook Club on a Sunday afternoon in 1957 when I won the first of my two Alabama Amateur Golf championships on a course that he was instrumental in creating. Fortunately in 1958 in Mobile I was able

Club fetes past presidents

First annual Presidents' Dinner at Birmingham Country Club Saturday night was a festive turnout. Honor guests were past presidents of the club, which was organized in 1898. Robert Jemison Jr., center, is the club's oldest living past president. Shown with him are, left to right, Bew White Jr., immediate past president; Mrs. White, Mrs. Elbert Jemison Jr. and Elbert Jemison Jr., current president. Dancing followed the dinner.

Sharing presidential salutes: Uncle and nephew shared recognition on this 1961 occasion when Country Club of Birmingham presidents were honored. Robert Jemison, Jr., (center) was recognized as the club's oldest living past president. On his right are immediate past president Bew White and Mrs. White. On his left are Elbert Jemison, Jr., then president, and Mrs. Jemison. (Courtesy The Birmingham News; *clipping rephotographed for this book)*

to repeat as state champion, but he had to applaud that one from afar.

I was especially pleased that Uncle Bob came with Dad to be present at the 1961 annual meeting of the Country Club of Birmingham when I was elected president. He, too, had been president in 1917, 10 years prior to the beginning of the

Mountain Brook Club. At the 1961 meeting he was honored as the club's oldest surviving past president.

I was fortunate indeed to have had an uncle like Robert Jemison, Jr.

I never felt that I was Uncle Bob's favorite nephew. To my knowledge he had no favorites; he was equally fond of all nieces and nephews. He did tell me that he was proud of my accomplishments, but I heard him make similar remarks to other family members.

VI.
Remembering His Confidants

We all know that successful people have close friends or family members who provide guidance, inspiration and motivation. This is certainly true of business-career successes.

Such was the career of Robert Jemison, Jr. When Uncle Bob died in 1974 I was much younger, of course. But I still vividly recall many of his "confidants." Not all of them were business-related.

I have compiled an alphabetical list of the people I remember as his confidants. Undoubtedly there were others, perhaps including longtime employees at Spring Lake Farms and Jemison Realty Co., all of them valued friends. Understand that I couldn't possibly have known them all. I remember many.

TOM BARTEE, for several decades vice president and corporate secretary of Jemison Realty Co. Thus most administration came across his desk.

CHARLOTTE CUSICK. For more than half a century Miss Cusick was Uncle Bob's loyal secretary. She did all his typing, filed all personal and business matters and produced scrapbooks reflecting his honors.

Her lifespan paralleled Uncle Bob's as she was near his age, 96, when he died in 1974 after becoming ill at his office.

Miss Cusick was loved by all of Uncle Bob's business-associated friends and family members.

HILL FERGUSON married Louise Walker, Uncle Bob's sister-in-law. At the University of Alabama prior to Uncle Bob's transfer to Sewanee, he and Ferguson became close friends and renewed the close association at Jemison Realty Co. He

Uncle Bob with Hill Ferguson, fellow student at the University of Alabama, fellow officer at Jemison Realty and diligent history researcher. (Courtesy, Dave Mace, Birmingham Association of Realtors).

was a vice president of the company and an Alabama history scholar.

HENRY GRAHAM was much younger, thus Uncle Bob met him later than he met many of his confidants. Because Henry wanted to be in real estate development, he chose Jemison Realty. He became a valued associate and loyal, dedicated friend of Uncle Bob, who made him a vice-president.

Later Henry formed his own highly successful real estate firm. He also became a major-general in the Alabama National Guard and commanded the 31st Division. He was in command when the division was federalized by President Kennedy and was ordered to Tuscaloosa when Gov. Wallace made his highly publicized schoolhouse-door stand.

Henry told me several times, "Your Uncle Bob meant so very much to me, for which I am grateful."

DR. ALEX GUERRY. When Dr. Guerry became vice chancellor of the University of the South (Sewanee), a close friendship with Uncle Bob commenced. They shared beliefs and traditions that were

Dr. Alex Guerry (Courtesy, Sewanee Alumni News)

and are a part of Sewanee.

I had the privilege of knowing Dr. Guerry during my three years at Sewanee Military Academy, which was a part of the university. A day I will never forget was Monday, June 3, 1940, graduation day. Dr. Guerry presented me the United States Army Officer Sabre, symbolic of the Sevier Award, as the academy's outstanding cadet of the class of 1940.

A giant among leaders, he passed away much too early. Born on Oct. 17, 1890, he died Oct. 19, 1948 at age 58.

ELBERT S. JEMISON, my father, was associated with Uncle Bob all the latter's business career. He was a Jemison Realty vice president and for many years was sales manager. The two worked closely in development of Redmont and Mountain Brook. Because they were brothers, they had a unique relationship, each having a deep interest in real estate. Their devotion to each other was equally beneficial.

Elbert Jemison, Sr.

*Virginia Walker Jemison
(Courtesy, Weesie G. Smith).*

VIRGINIA WALKER JEMISON was Uncle Bob's caring partner throughout their lifelong love affair. After she died, he continued to carry the torch of love and devotion.

JOHN (JACK) PERSONS, longtime president of the First National Bank of Birmingham, now AmSouth. As a National Guard major-general he commanded the 31st Division in the Pacific Theater in World War Two. He was a financial adviser and a source of financing for Uncle Bob's personal and business needs. They were close personal friends.

H.G. "DIDDY" SEIBELS. A lasting, very close friendship started when he and Uncle Bob were students at Sewanee. In later years when Uncle Bob was forming Jemison Realty Co.,

Seibels was developing Jemison-Seibels Insurance Co., which occupied the second floor of the Jemison Building at Third Avenue and 21st Street North.

Along with their devoted friendship the two shared a business relationship over many decades. The Jemison and Seibels families have long been closely-knit.

Diddy Seibels was captain of the 1899 Sewanee football team that shut out five major opponents in six days on the road. And I must note this: Seibels won the Alabama amateur golf championship in 1922.

ALFRED SHOOK, prominent financier, helped organize an early Birmingham bank. He and Uncle Bob were close friends many years and my uncle often called on Shook for guidance.

Golfers and confidants Henry G. "Diddy" Seibels,
Gen. Jack Persons, Herbert Tutwiler, Alfred Shook.
(Courtesy, Doug Shook)

HERBERT TUTWILER was associated with Uncle Bob in construction of major buildings in downtown Birmingham. They shared love of and devotion to the Episcopal Church of the Advent, now a cathedral and home of the Alabama Diocese.

After Jemison Realty and Uncle Bob built the beautiful Mount Vernon Colonial-style model home on Mountain Brook Parkway, Tutwiler purchased it. As a close friend of his son, Temple W. Tutwiler II, I enjoyed many visits there.

THE REV. JOHN C. TURNER, rector of the Episcopal Church of the Advent. In 1940 at age 33 he gave the commencement sermon in All Saints Chapel at Sewanee at my Sewanee Military Academy graduation.

The Rev. John Turner (Courtesy, Betsy Turner Allison)

John Turner was much younger than Uncle Bob, who was 62 in 1940, but the two molded a lasting, devoted association. He was more than Uncle Bob's preacher at the Advent, he was a valued friend, a very special and caring person. Members of all ages called him "Uncle John." He wanted that.

He was born Jan. 14, 1907 and died Aug. 30, 1966 at the much-too-early-age of 59. That was an extraordinarily sad time for Advent members as he was loved by all. I wondered again, as I did in combat in Europe, why do the good die young?

Personal note: After I returned home from Europe at the end of World War Two, Uncle John Turner asked me to consider entering theological school to prepare for the ministry. I thanked him for the honor and confidence, but I was considering a career in professional golf or the Regular Army. Ultimately I chose neither.

A.H. "RICK" WOODWARD, Uncle Bob's brother-in-law as he married Annie Jemison, Uncle Bob's sister and my aunt.

*A. H. (Rick) Woodward
(Courtesy A.H. (Rick)
Woodward III)*

Uncle Bob and Uncle Rick were close brothers-in-law as they shared optimism and progressive thinking. Uncle Rick was president of Woodward Iron Co., builder of Rickwood baseball field, preserved today as America's oldest baseball stadium. He was an early owner of the Birmingham Barons baseball team.

The home he built for his family was given to the University of Alabama at Birmingham and is the Woodward House for UAB presidents.

On a personal note: I feel that Uncle Rick should be in the Alabama Sports Hall of Fame for his contributions to base-ball.

Through the years many persons have told me what a memo-rable and helpful influence Uncle Bob was on their careers. Recently my longtime and valued friend Philip Jackson, Jr., told me something I hadn't known until then.

Phil said that when he entered the real estate and mortgage business in 1949, Uncle Bob told him that, due to national economic downturns, he was entering a risky business, and that everyone in the business was subject to going broke, per-haps even facing bankruptcy.

Uncle Bob suggested that he do things for his community that would last, and that if he did run into financial problems, he would be able to see the good that he had done.

Phil also told me of Uncle Bob's association with William

P.G. Harding, who was president of Birmingham's First National Bank, now AmSouth, and later was chairman of the Federal Reserve Board.

Mr. Harding told Uncle Bob that as Birmingham did not have a major cemetery, he would lend him the money to develop one. Uncle Bob accepted his suggestion and Elmwood Cemetery resulted.

In 1927, two years before the economic crash, Mr. Harding told Uncle Bob to sell his assets and revert to cash. Uncle Bob did not do so but later said he wished he had.

Phil Jackson, Jr., became a highly successful real estate and mortgage executive and served on the Federal Reserve Board under President Gerald R. Ford.

VII.

Real Estate Rookie

Having earned a diploma at the University of the South, Sewanee, Robert Jemison, Jr., stood at the proverbial crossroads. That was 1899, many years before baseball's Yogi Berra would advise: "When you come to a fork in the road, take it."

Uncle Bob may have known the fork he intended taking, but I don't think family records mention it. What is on record is that he immediately began work as a clerk at Prowell Hardware in still-new Birmingham.

He stayed in the hardware job three years, then he made known the "fork" he surely had planned in college years to take: He organized Jemison Real Estate and Insurance Co. and opened for business Jan. 1, 1903.

Why real estate? We don't have it in writing, but I will surmise: It was in his Jemison genes. He had looked at infant Birmingham and saw the need and the opportunity for land development. His father had demonstrated intelligence and resourcefulness in helping provide the new city electric power and public transportation.

I would think that Uncle Bob surely had often talked land development with his father, who soon after moving to Birmingham had shared in the purchase of East Lake Land Co. Uncle Bob's decision to study mining engineering at the University of Alabama would fit naturally into his plans to be a land developer in Birmingham, bordered on its south side by mountainous terrain.

So when he made his initial move into real estate, Robert Jemison, Jr., had made a firm, clear, planned choice. Apparently he never looked back.

The very next year, 1904, he was appointed agent for sale of Ensley Highlands property by owner Robert A. Terrell. Also in 1904 he was appointed agent for and supervised development of Earle Place for Judge Samuel E. Greene and family.

In 1905 Uncle Bob organized Central Park Land Co. and developed the Central Park subdivision on Birmingham's western side. That same year he organized and served as president of the Redmont Land Co., a group of companies that developed major subdivisions.

Birmingham merchants decided in 1906 that they needed a strong central voice to promote their interests, and they established the Birmingham Commercial Club, soon renamed the Birmingham Chamber of Commerce. And who better to head the club than the up-and-coming young real estate leader, Robert Jemison, Jr., now 28?

Robert Jemison, Jr. in his early years as a realtor. (Courtesy, family collection)

On June 30, 1907 Jemison Realty opened the Mountain Terrace subdivision.

And in 1909 Jemison Realty organized the Corey Land Co. with Robert Jemison, Jr., as president. The company developed the town of Corey, soon renamed Fairfield. And that auspicious event merits full attention in the Robert Jemison, Jr., story.

Uncle Bob had a hand in development of numerous Birmingham landmarks, among them the Ridgely Apartments at Sixth Avenue and 21st Street North, considered the best of early Birmingham apartments. Herbert Tutwiler was the primary developer.

Many decades later, after the city's once-prestigious Tutwiler Hotel was dismantled, the Ridgely was renamed the Tutwiler.

Realtor Robert Jemison, Jr. (back row, fourth from left) with crew starting work on the Ridgely Apartments. (Courtesy, the Birmingham Public Library)

Tutwiler Hotel today, formerly the Ridgely Apartments.

VIII.

Fairfield – Theodore Roosevelt Applauds Uncle Bob

In the early years of the 20th Century when Birmingham was staking its claim to being "Pittsburgh of the South," Robert Jemison, Jr., made a truly noteworthy contribution to the area. The United States Steel Corporation, having acquired the Birmingham-based Tennessee Coal and Iron Co., purchased large tracts of land nearby to be used for industrial expansion and commercial and residential development.

U.S. Steel previously had experimented, with only limited success, in financing construction of milltown communities for employees. Now the steel giant hoped to attract private financing of a new town near its plants west of Birmingham.

In 1909 U.S. Steel asked a delegation of Birmingham area businessmen to New York to discuss its proposal for the new town that was to be financed, planned, constructed and supervised by Birmingham businesses.

The delegation response was positive and the person deemed best qualified to plan the new town was realtor Robert Jemison, Jr., who by now had made a name for himself in Birmingham area real estate.

Uncle Bob agreed to take on the U.S. Steel project. On

63

Nov. 5, 1909, with eight other area businessmen, he organized the Corey Land Co. (The then-town name, Corey, honored U.S. Steel's second president).

A site comprising 256 1/2 acres (where Fairfield now stands) was acquired and Uncle Bob then toured what were considered the best-designed industrial towns in the United States and Europe. After the tour he searched for a gifted person to design the town that at first would be called Corey. His choice was a nationally recognized architect, George H. Miller of Boston.

Together on foot, Jemison and Miller thoroughly examined the proposed town site, noting all facets of the landscape. Then Miller returned to Boston and produced his design. As described by Marvin Y. Whiting in his fine book *FAIRFIELD. . .Past. Present. Future*, the town roads would curve gently up and around slopes, and Miller's design would maximize the variety of both topography and the plantings of more than 100,000 trees, shrubs and flowers.

Every lot in the town would have a sanitary outlet, with gas and water mains, electrical conduit and telephone connections, and all streets would be guttered and curbed, Whiting wrote. Building restrictions were specified for all business and residential lots.

In brief, architect Miller—with Robert Jemison Jr. and associates figuratively looking over his shoulder—had designed

Former President Theodore Roosevelt invited Uncle Bob and other Birmingham area leaders to accompany him as he toured Fairfield, the model milltown U.S. Steel had employed Uncle Bob to develop. Roosevelt is shaking hands with Charles W. Lutz, superintendent of American Steel and Wire Co.Uncle Bob (hat in hand) talks to a greeter by the car. (Courtesy, the Birmingham Library Archives)

the town to be attractive and livable. Provisions were made for parks, public buildings and commercial areas. Fairfield was praised as the model mill town, including positive comment by a later-visiting former president, Theodore Roosevelt.

Prospective homeowners were highly pleased, as evidenced by their purchases of home sites from Jemison's Corey Land Co.

When Roosevelt came to Birmingham in March 1911 as a delegate to the National Child Labor Conference, he toured Corey and in a speech there praised the new town as "simply extraordinary." Later with his touring party back in Birmingham he spoke at Capitol Park and again spoke highly of Corey.

Then, prior to a luncheon at the Hillman Hotel once again he was asked about Corey. His response, as quoted in Marvin Whiting's book: "It is a great work. It strikes me as being in every way a model city. It will have a large bearing on social and industrial problems. By George, young Jemison, who is at the head of the Corey movement, is a corker!" (his presumed definition: one who excels).

Uncle Bob and a few other people had been privileged to ride with the former president (see photo) as he toured Corey in an open car. Sometimes I've wondered if he happened to share with Roosevelt his life creed as expressed by Daniel Webster. Thus, Corey, later to be renamed Fairfield, came to life and Robert Jemison, Jr., through his Corey Land Co., was a major force in giving it birth.

IX.

Redmont – A Sight to See

Thus far in these reflections on Uncle Bob Jemison's role in Birmingham's first century, he has developed neighborhoods to the city's north, east, south, west.

Looking back now, I feel certain that all along he was waiting for the appropriate time to make another move south, to and atop Red Mountain, then beyond. I refer to the mountain crest and both slopes, north and south.

Almost from the beginning of his land-development career, he was known as a visionary, someone who could clearly foresee the best possible use of land, small acreage and large.

I mentioned earlier in this text that Jemison brothers Robert and Elbert (my dad) worked side by side at Jemison Realty, thus knew each other's thinking, especially as that thinking pertained to real estate, their day-to-day business.

As I record these memories of Uncle Bob's long, productive career, I recall hearing some of their conversations about the workaday world of real estate. Because our family home was in Redmont, I remember that they conferred frequently about goings-on in that growing community. I certainly don't suggest that I knew the significance of what they were saying.

The Elbert Jemison home at 3525 Lenox Road was one of the first houses on the street, built in 1927.

Looking back now, I realize that my father and uncle may have considered the possibility of one day nudging me toward a future in real estate. But the fact that Uncle Bob sometimes was behind the 8-ball financially because of heavy real estate investments during the depression probably convinced them that I should enter another field.

Unlike the communities he had developed earlier, Uncle Bob had company in developing Redmont, principally Hill Ferguson, a valued associate at Jemison Realty, and members of the Henry Key Milner family.

The A.H. "Rick" Woodward home in Redmont, later home to presidents of the University of Alabama at Birmingham. (Courtesy, the Birmingham Library Archives)

As many readers will remember, during its heyday (about 1911 to 1935) Redmont Park was *the* place for affluent people to live in the Birmingham area. Many who had come to budding Birmingham had accumulated fortunes and wanted to live in an upscale neighborhood. They bought land and built opulent homes in Redmont.

According to a historical marker at Key Circle, the Redmont neighborhood included Alabama's finest collection of residential architecture of that era. Further, the marker states, "the area includes the state's best examples of the domestic use of Tudor, Spanish Revival, Classical Revival, English Cottage, Dutch Revival, Chateauesque, and Renaissance."

My chief purpose in this limited description of Redmont Park and adjacent areas is to include Uncle Bob's continuing involvement in the development of Birmingham. For anyone wishing the full story of Redmont, I recommend Cathy Adams' excellent book, *Worthy of Remembrance: A History of Redmont.*

X.

Mountain Brook – The Crown Jewel

Next came Mountain Brook, the crown jewel in Robert Jemison, Jr.'s real estate career.

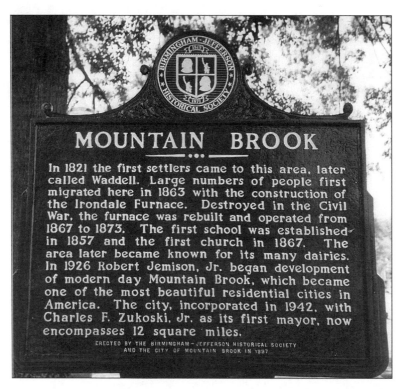

In 1821 the first settlers came to this area, later called Waddell. Large numbers of people first migrated here in 1863 with the construction of the Irondale Furnace. Destroyed in the Civil War, the furnace was rebuilt and operated from 1867 to 1873. The first school was established in 1857 and the first church in 1867. The area later became known for its many dairies. In 1926 Robert Jemison, Jr. began development of modern day Mountain Brook, which became one of the most beautiful residential cities in America. The city, incorporated in 1942, with Charles F. Zukoski, Jr. as its first mayor, now encompasses 12 square miles.

ERECTED BY THE BIRMINGHAM – JEFFERSON HISTORICAL SOCIETY
AND THE CITY OF MOUNTAIN BROOK IN 1997

Marker at Mountain Brook City Hall

For readers anticipating a history of the area that ultimately became Mountain Brook and nearby neighborhoods, I remind that Marilyn Davis Barefield covered that subject well in *A*

History of Mountain Brook, Alabama. I recommend her book for historical and geographical details.

What I propose for this portion of Uncle Bob's career is a capsule view of how he undertook the overall development of Mountain Brook. Not only the many handsome residences on spacious sites, but also the planned commercial areas, public buildings, recreation areas that would feature two golf clubs with nationally recognized courses, public parks and a riding academy with attractive trails. Plus, of course, public utilities. And as a kind of clincher, Uncle Bob would offer his recommendations on how the new city should be governed, policed and provided fire protection.

As has been noted, he had a gift for looking at undeveloped land and envisioning its completed potential. I can imagine him standing atop Red Mountain, gazing south and anticipating the beautiful neighborhood he would develop. Chances are, he stood there many times and envisioned the city-to-be.

Beautiful Mountain Brook model home, resembling Washington's Mt. Vernon; built by Jemison Realty Co.

In 1926 he and associates began developing the 250-acre Mountain Brook Estates and followed by establishing the 2,000-acre Mountain Brook Land Co.

Perhaps more than ever in Uncle Bob's dream development, his determination to preserve the land as he found it came into play. The terrain was ideal, and, as Mountain Brook history author Barefield noted, he "used the best landscape artists and city planners available and was ahead of his time in his designs for the major street arteries and winding roadways."

Many decades after Uncle Bob's dedicated development task, Mountain Brook is, I am often reminded, one of the most beautiful, best-planned communities in this country. Past and present citizens have paid tribute to Uncle Bob in varied ways, most notably in establishment of Robert Jemison Park and in posting two impressive road markers (photos in next chapter).

Because I have been immersed in golf most of my life, it's obvious why I think first of the magnificent golf courses for which Uncle Bob was responsible. And this is an appropriate place to spotlight another remarkable point about him: He did not have to be personally involved in an activity to recognize its value to the community.

For example, he did not play golf, yet his foresight and vision about overall land development led directly to construction of two excellent 18-hole courses at the Country Club of

Birmingham and another at Mountain Brook Club. He knew what those three courses would mean to the people of Mountain Brook and by extension to Greater Birmingham and Alabama. He recognized that golf was great outdoor recreation in an attractive environment.

Because Uncle Bob wanted the three courses to be among the finest in America, he brought in the man recognized as the best golf course designer available, Scotland's Donald Ross, then living in Pinehurst, N.C. Ross ultimately designed more than 600 courses in this country and abroad.

Pardon a personal note. The two courses on which I later would win back-to-back Alabama amateur championships were Ross-designed—Mountain Brook in 1957 and Mobile Country Club in 1958. Uncle Bob told me after each that he

Donald Ross, world-famed golf course designer whom Uncle Bob retained to plan the three courses in Mountain Brook. (Courtesy, Given Memorial Library, Tufts Archives, Pinehurst, N.C.)

DONALD J. ROSS
Golf Course Construction and Architecture
Little Compton, Rhode Island

Pinehurst, N. C.
Associates: March 22, 1929

Walter B. Hatch
N. Amherst, Mass.

J. B. McGovern
Wynnewood, Pa.

Mr. Robert Jemison, Jr.
The Jemison Companies
Birmingham, Alabama

Dear Mr.Jemison:

        The Mountain Brook Golf Course is laid out on property
which has many unusual and attractive features. Many of the holes
are laid out through valleys, other cross meadow leans through
which a creek runs forming many natural hazards. Many of the
holes are cut through solid forest which gives very pleasant
landscape effects.

        No attempt has been made to make the course a difficult
one; rather was it designed to give the maximum amount of pleasure
to the average golfer, at the same time giving the scratch player
many problems to negotiate. Tees are large, so the course is
adjustable in length from 6,100 yards to 6,300 yards and the
par is as follows:

#1 - 4, #2 - 4, #3 - 4, #4 - 3, #5 - 5, #6 - 4, #7 - 3, #8 - 4,
#9 - 5, out 36, #10 - 4, #11 - 5, #12 - 4, #13 - 4, #14 - 4,
#15 - 3, #16 - 4, #17 - 3, #18 - 4, In 35, Total 71.

        The course is one of unusual beauty and the holes
have character and individuality.

        The club house is situated in a pine grove overlooking
tee #1, green #18, practice green and practice field. At a convenient distance is a park containing many beautiful specimens
of trees and vones. The whole setting is one of great attraction.

                              Yours very truly,

                              / S / Donald J. Ross

Copy: Mr. Morton
      Mr. Hanson
      Mr. Ramsay
      Mr. Crawford

was delighted I had won the championship, and I'm sure he was pleased that he had had an indirect hand in my winning. I was fortunate to win a number of tournaments on another Ross jewel, the West course of the Country Club of Birmingham, where numerous Alabama and Southern championships have been played.

The East course is another shining example of Donald Ross's work. It is one of my favorite courses, as it is for many golfers of varying abilities. Through the years it has undergone remodeling projects, but the enjoyable, comfortable-to-play classic designs have been preserved. Each green is near the next tee. It is a course where what you see is what you get, and you get what you see.

Uncle Bob described to Ross what he wanted in course design, stressing his wish to disturb as little as possible what nature had provided so bountifully.

Mountain Brook Club

The Country Club of Birmingham (Courtesy, Shannon Rumage and The Country Club of Birmingham).

Probably no other municipality in America has two such outstanding clubs as Mountain Brook Club and the Country Club of Birmingham, founded in Birmingham in 1898.

In 2004 the Mountain Brook course was restored, using the concept and many of the original designs of 1929 by Donald Ross. The course stood the test of time, providing enjoyment for all golf abilities. The marker yardage in 1929 was 6,300; today it is only 202 yards longer, playing to the same enjoyment and characteristics as when built in 1929.

In 1943 when I was at Camp Butner, N.C., I went to Pinehurst, N.C., to play in the North-South Open before going to Europe with the 35th Division. While at Pinehurst I phoned Mr. Ross, hoping to see him. He invited me to his home and a memorable visit followed.

I recall that he told me that Uncle Bob had explained to him that the Mountain Brook Club Planning Committee wanted a golf course that would be enjoyable to play by all members and guests regardless of their abilities. That criterion has not changed.

Uncle Bob's foresight has rewarded Mountain Brook in innumerable ways along with the residential and commercial layouts. One enormous benefit has been city government—an unsalaried mayor and council, but with a paid professional city manager.

Through the years the arrangement has assured Mountain Brook excellent leadership by men and women with talent and devotion to the city, serving without compensation and without political wrangling.

I think Uncle Bob would be delighted with Mountain Brook's all-around success story and its continuing image as one of America's prettiest and best-planned suburbs, possessing such outstanding municipal departments as police, fire, court system, park board and a truly fine library that averages 20,000 visitors a month.

The school system ranks among the best in America in all categories. I do wish that the high school offered ROTC (reserve officer training corps) as I favor that training of our youth.

A few things in Mountain Brook that would displease Uncle

*Elbert Jemison, Jr.
nephew of the man
responsible for the
Mountain Brook
Riding Academy,
aboard his pony
about 1930.*

*David Thurlow, Eugene Yates, on their ponies along Shades
Creek, 1929. (Courtesy, David Thurlow).*

Bob are speeding cars, drivers ignoring stop signs, drivers talking on cell phones, driving dangerously close to the car in front, others not stopping for pedestrians in crosswalks, still others not using turn indicators and not turning on their lights when needed. Perhaps most of all, he would be saddened that his Mountain Brook now needs a jail!

For me, one of Uncle Bob's key contributions to Mountain Brook was its riding academy. I had to refresh my memory on the academy's features, which some readers may recall: 60 horse stalls, a blacksmith shop and staff veterinarian.

Having noticed increased riding interest in Birmingham, Uncle Bob felt certain that a riding academy would find wide

The Old Mill, long a favorite Mountain Brook attraction; Uncle Bob updated it and added a tearoom.

favor in Mountain Brook. It did. I well remember fun rides with my dad on Sunday afternoons.

In keeping with Uncle Bob's knack of planning for the future, the riding trails were placed where roads ultimately would be. Riding trails are still evident, especially along Overbrook Road and the second hole of Mountain Brook golf course.

Another Uncle Bob attraction was the restored Old Mill on the Shades Creek site of a former working mill. A tea room enhanced its drawing power. The Old Mill was across the roadway, now Mountain Brook Parkway, from a model home that closely resembles George Washington's Mount Vernon. It remains a favorite Mountain Brook viewing attraction.

After it was built as a "model home," the residence's first owner was the Herbert Tutwiler family. As Temple Tutwiler was a close friend, I spent several nights in his home. Later we were fellow cadets at Sewanee Military Academy, then fellow students at the University of Virginia prior to our going to Europe in World War Two.

It's no secret that Uncle Bob was widely admired. I could recite printed compliments from a host of friends, but I will mention only one of my favorites, Dr. Henry Edmonds, noted Birmingham clergyman and newspaper columnist.

Dr. Edmonds once mentioned "the difficult and intricate manipulations that were required...to put across his (Uncle

Bob's) developments." Then he added, "Always Mr. Jemison was suffering reverses and getting up to try again. Always he was doing the kind of thing that did not make money, but made beauty."

As for me, I did not believe that Uncle Bob's purpose in life was to make money. He developed Mountain Brook and other areas to provide people a great place to live. I have heard people say, "He had no enemies, but he had a world of respect."

Today, because of the higher value of Mountain Brook homesites, property taxes and homeowners' insurance premiums are very expensive. In my opinion a possible problem for Mountain Brook is the fact that the uncontrollable expenses are escalating faster than homeowners' income. That is especially true for retirees. People who will not have adequate cash flow will have to move to less expensive sites. Such a development certainly would have disturbed Uncle Bob.

XI.

Jemison Park—A Lasting Tribute

Of the many honors and accolades bestowed on Uncle Bob, I think one he most cherished is Friends of Jemison Park, the living memorial in his beloved Mountain Brook which that organization established.

For readers who need a reminder, Jemison Park extends about two miles along Mountain Brook Parkway and Overbrook Road paralleling Shades Creek and also along Cahaba Road adjacent to Watkins Creek.

The Friends' booklet *A Brief History of Jemison Park* includes this: "When Mountain Brook was subdivided, the developers reserved these lands from adjacent estates to be preserved in their natural estates as a park of plants such as William Bartram found in the Southeast on the eve of the Revolution."

Because Uncle Bob was so committed to preserving the natural beauty of the areas he developed, this passage from the incorporation of "Friends of Jemison Park" surely pleased him immensely:

"To preserve and protect the natural attraction of Robert

Robert Jemison, Jr., developer of Mountain Brook Estates, is shown with a marker that was erected in his honor at Cahaba Road and Mountain Brook Parkway during 1953. The park was named for Mr. Jemison by the City of Mountain Brook and the marker was provided by his friends and family.

Jemison Park (in Mountain Brook, Alabama), to encourage its use by walkers, bicyclists, and those interested in the study of natural history, to conserve its natural resources, and to preserve its conservational, scenic, esthetic and parkland values."

As Uncle Bob truly was a people person, he was elated that the members of Friends of Jemison Park were friends of his and family members who lived in Mountain Brook and shared his beliefs about the community.

I know that he enjoyed attending the Friends' annual meetings, always held at a member's home, and the social atmosphere. Another aspect that pleased him was knowing that Jemison Park would continue for generations.

The Friends of Jemison Park organization has been most fortunate in having the dedication and expertise of Thomas N. Carruthers, one of Alabama's outstanding attorneys. Also, gratitude is hereby expressed to founders, presidents and past and present board members.

Founders, not a formally organized group, included Rucker Agee, "Weesie" Smith, Bob and Elberta Reid, George and Isabelle Maynard, Dale and Tom Carruthers. I salute them, for Uncle Bob and for the extended Jemison family, for originating the Friends of Jemison Park project.

The following persons have served as president: Thomas N. Carruthers, George F. Maynard, Lowell Hamilton, John Goff, Bill Cothran, Roy Shivers, Elna Shugarman, Nimrod Long, Russell Bailey, Robin O'Neal and Sally Worthen.

Initial board members were Rucker Agee, J. Russell Bailey, Thomas N. Carruthers, Ed M. Friend, Jr., Larry Hamilton, George F. Maynard, Henry D. McHenry, M. Camper O'Neal, Robert R. Reid, Jr., Elberta Reid, Lindsay C. Smith and Louise G. Smith.

Subsequent board members: Emory Cunningham, Louise Gale, John Goff, Jackie Monaghan, Robin O'Neal, Margaret

Porter, Roy Shivers, Elna Shugarman, Elmer Thuston, Jr., Louise Wrinkle, Sally Worthen, Jess Ann Jemison, Anne J. Heppenstall and possibly others.

Several original organizers of Jemison Park have said that Kirkman O'Neal was a valued supporter of the project. As his home was on Mountain Brook Parkway, he had a keen interest in the park. More important, he wanted to support a project that would be an asset to the community. He and Uncle Bob maintained a long and valued friendship.

Mayor Zukoski (right) and the honoree as Jemison Park is dedicated. (Courtesy, The Birmingham, News*).*

Because remarks made Oct. 8, 1952 at the dedication of the park pay wonderful and permanent tribute to Uncle Bob, I present them here. The mayor and City Council's formal resolution, passed earlier, had noted that the Mountain Brook area "owes its preeminence as a residential district primarily to the enterprise, foresight, enthusiasm and fundamental good taste of one man, Robert Jemison, Jr."

And, the resolution concluded, a copy would be sent to Uncle Bob "as an evidence of the admiration and affection of the citizens of Mountain Brook for him and of their deep appreciation of his vision and courage in the development of the Mountain Brook area."

Now I return to the remarks made at the park dedication:

"We are here to do honor to a good and a great man. It is fitting that we should do so, especially while he is living and continues so actively with his life's work.

"The monument to this man is to be seen all about us. This park is but one aspect of it, a beautiful and personal little spot, left as nature made it, which we can keep and nurture as a perpetual reminder of him and of his place in our ranks. But in a larger sense, all Birmingham and all of its environs are his monument, because there he has done and is doing his work and there are the tangible evidences of his life's contributions."

"I would like to have you travel in your mind's eye around the Birmingham district with me to see what this man has done. Let's start on Twentieth Street in downtown Birmingham. There at the corner of First Avenue is the Empire Building. A block down at Nineteenth Street is the old Chamber of Commerce Building. A block up at Twenty-first Street is the Birmingham Electric Building. All of these are the result of his handiwork, his vision and his faith in Jones Valley.

"Walk a few blocks north to Fifth and Sixth avenues and see the Tutwiler Hotel and the Ridgely Apartments, these and other downtown structures, which are landmarks of Birmingham, would probably never have seen the light of day but for him.

"But this man's vision was more on where people live than for where they work. Travel out west to Fairfield and there you will see a lovely residential area called Corey, which he laid out and developed a great many years ago. Skip over to Central Park, to Mountain Terrace, to Redmont Park, all of these are memorials to the man who saw early the possibilities of diffused and outlying places for living, where men and women and their children might enjoy trees and flowers and open spaces every day of their existence, provided they were given neighborhoods large enough, and lots of adequate size, and carefully planned improvements, and reasonable restrictions on land use.

"This man's crowning glory was and is his ability to dream dreams of order and spaciousness and beauty, and to translate those dreams into reality. He is a man possessed of the spirit and the quiet determination to see that what we build for our community is governed by the things of the spirit as well as by material things. Preeminently above all of our citizens he stood and stands for grace and beauty in daily living and his influence has been immense.

"Those of us who are here today and who live within easy dis-

Picturebook walk in Jemison Park.

tance of this park owe this man a debt of gratitude. For here it was that he conceived and created his masterpiece. In all the land there is no better designed or executed residential area than the original Mountain Brook survey. Taking every advantage of the superb natural resources which were at hand, this man created here a symphony of winding roads and lovely homes, set in a background of trees and slopes, the pride and joy of all who live there and the desire of all who do not.

"There he recognized, too, that recreation and education have their important place in everyday existence, and planned and provided a school, a country club, a natural park, and other facilities which mean more and more to our people every day.

89

"The Mountain Brook Club is a gem among clubs of America. The Mountain Brook School was set down in a generous 10-acre area of ideal topography and location and at this moment is being extended and completed according to the original plan which this man devised.

"The park lands along this branch at our side and along Shades Creek from Cahaba to Beechwood Road contain natural flowing water and trees and native shrubs which some day we will find the means to develop as they deserve. And the example of this man's ideal and highest achievement has spread to influence every other area in what we now call the City of Mountain Brook and far beyond."

(Note: The next several paragraphs of the dedication remarks capsuled Uncle Bob's birth in Tuscaloosa, the family's move to Birmingham and his schooling—information provided at the start of this account. But I include now the final remarks).

"Mr. Jemison, we are here to honor you for a life well-lived, the noblest achievement of which a man is capable. We respect and we love you for all you have done and for all you are, for your humility, for your modesty, for your cheerful optimism, for the light of your eyes and of your smile, for your wistful reflection, for your wisdom and your undaunted courage. You have succeeded far beyond the lot of most men in doing for your fellow man and you have gained the high plateau of character and example for which your life will encourage us to strive."

XII.
Realtor of the Century!

January 14, 1972 was indeed a red-letter day for the Birmingham Board of Realtors. On that day the board proudly proclaimed one of its members, Robert Jemison, Jr., "Realtor of the Century." Presumably the accolade meant "for Birmingham," but the board's burst of pride that day could have been aimed at the entire country!

The Birmingham Realtors supported their superlative with "evidence." Member John D. Chichester spoke in glowing tribute to Uncle Bob, reciting his colorful and productive career as Birmingham Realtor, starting in a one-room office in the Woodward Building and culminating in the development of Mountain Brook.

In between, Chichester recounted, the honoree had developed Central Park, Ensley Highlands, Mountain Terrace, Forest Park, Redmont and other communities. U.S. Steel Corp., aware of his skills, had chosen Uncle Bob to develop its model mill town, Fairfield.

He had served as first and youngest Birmingham Chamber of Commerce president and led community fund drives. He had served as president of the Birmingham Real Estate Board and in 1926 was chosen to head the National Real Estate Board, Chichester recalled. And in 1934 he was appointed Alabama's first Federal Housing Administrator.

On and on, Uncle Bob's accomplishments were cited. Then the Birmingham Real Estate Board played its ace, proclaiming him "Realtor of the Century." Board President Wallace Boothby presented Uncle Bob a plaque that so proclaimed.

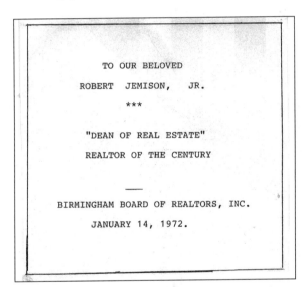

TO OUR BELOVED

ROBERT JEMISON, JR.

***

"DEAN OF REAL ESTATE"
REALTOR OF THE CENTURY

———

BIRMINGHAM BOARD OF REALTORS, INC.
JANUARY 14, 1972.

This is a copy of its program front the day the Birmingham Real Estate Board saluted Robert Jemison, Jr., proclaiming him "Realtor of the Century."

The board's tribute included these words: "It is not only a personal pleasure, but a considered privilege to have opportunity in behalf of the Birmingham Board of Realtors to pay tribute and honor to a most distinguished citizen, an honorary (member) of this board and a past president of the National Association of Real Estate Boards. A man who has contributed more to the development of the Birmingham district than anyone, and a man held high in the esteem of fellow citizens, and loved and respected by all. This reference is to Robert Jemison, Jr.

Later, in conclusion: "Bob, we all love and respect you. We are all proud of your many accomplishments in developing Birmingham and bringing many honors to the city.

"Your ambition on entering the real estate field in 1903 to build a 'bigger and better Birmingham' has been fulfilled to the letter. May there be many more Bob Jemisons.

"On the 28th day of February you will reach your 94th birthday. We all know it will be just another leaf in your life, bringing to you that vim, vigor and enthusiasm that you have possessed during the past 70 years. May God bless you."

The "Realtor of the Century" lived two years after that memorable day, literally active to his very last. He died at age 96, several hours after becoming ill in his office.

XIII.
Serving His Community

"Have you paid your civic rent?"

That question was posed to Birmingham citizens by a community leader decades ago. I resurrect it here because it reminds me of Robert Jemison, Jr., who paid his civic rent in spades. He would never have thought of it as "rent" but as further opportunity to serve his fellow man and community.

In researching his career in library files, I was astonished that, with the daily demands of his real estate career, he found time for innumerable volunteer community projects. In this account I note only the major ones.

Understandably, because Uncle Bob was a quick success in real estate, many of his volunteer roles were business-related. In 1906 he helped found the Birmingham Chamber of Commerce and served at age 28 as its first president. That year he also accepted the position of vice chairman of the Birmingham Park Commission.

Despite having attended the University of Alabama only his freshman and sophomore years, in 1907 he was elected president of the school alumni association.

In 1916 a Birmingham Chapter of the American Red Cross was established and Uncle Bob was chosen the body's first chairman. Also that year he was elected president of the Country Club of Birmingham.

Ever active on the school front, in 1922 he was chosen president of the Fathers Club of Hill School, Pottstown, Pa.

Having attended the University of the South, Sewanee, his junior and seniors years, in 1925 he was elected to the school's Board of Trustees. A year later he was named to the Board of Regents. As noted in an earlier chapter, for the remainder of his life he was one of Sewanee's most active supporters.

Nationally known on the real estate front, in 1926 he was elected president of the National Association of Real Estate Boards. That year he also became a member of the Board of Trustees of Alabama Hospitals and served the association 20 years.

In 1927 while serving as chairman of the Birmingham Community Chest (later known as the United Appeal), Uncle Bob invited world-famed Helen Keller, blind and deaf author/lecturer of Tuscumbia, to the organization's kickoff luncheon. Her letter of response to him, thanking him for his letter to her and for her visit, is printed in this chapter.

In 1932 Uncle Bob served on President Herbert Hoover's

Helen Keller (Courtesy the Birmingham Public Library).

Below:Symbolic of Robert Jemison, Jr.'s service to the Birmingham community is this letter to him from noted Alabamian Helen Keller. Miss Keller thanked him for inviting her to help launch Birmingham's annual Community Chest fund campaign. (Courtesy, Jemison family collection).

November 9, 1927.

Mr. Robert Jemison, General Chairman,
of the Committee of the Community Chest,
Birmingham, Alabama.

Dear Mr. Jemison:

    Before I settle down to work again after my
thrilling trip to "the magic city," I must yield to a
very strong impulse to thank you and the other members
of the Community Chest Committee for a delightful good
time. How kind and considerate you all were, smoothing
away difficulties and making of obstacles stepping-stones
to success.

    The meeting was splendid, and carried on its
face the smile of victory. As I stood before that great
audience, I sensed the warm heartbeats of Birmingham, and
I loved the attentive, responsive multitude.

    If I could put into my letter some of the southern
sunshine and fragrance and loveliness which filled my visit,
you would have an idea of my happy gratitude; but since
words are only words, I must leave unsaid my deepest emotions.
I can only hope that I have been a little useful to the
Community Chest, and that many substantial donations will
soon give power to its beneficent work. When more men like
you and your co-workers get together, most of the calamities
of mankind will be dissolved in the sunshine of a happier
civilization.

    With kind greetings to the Committee, and with warm
personal regards to yourself, in which Miss Thomson joins me,
I am,

                    Sincerely yours,
                    Helen Keller

P.S.   The afternoon post has just brought your letter. Many
thanks. I am immensely pleased with it, and very proud of the
undeserved praise you have heaped upon my humble efforts.

                H. K.

Conference on City Planning. Two years later he was appointed first director of the Federal Housing Authority in Alabama. In 1953 *Dixie Business* magazine presented him its Distinguished Service Award for his half century of developing Birmingham.

Uncle Bob and Aunt Virginia were dedicated members of the Episcopal Church of the Advent, formed in 1872, the year Birmingham itself was founded.

The church is on Sixth Avenue North between 20th and 21st streets. Uncle Bob's parents' home was on the southeast cor-

The Jemisons Jr. arrive for a community event. (Courtesy Caroline M. Jemison)

ner of Sixth Avenue and 21st Street; the church is on the southwest corner.

Five generations of the Jemison family have been active members of the Advent. In 1962 members dedicated Jemison Hall there. Uncle Bob was senior warden emeritus and Aunt Virginia served on numerous women's committees, especially the one on flower arrangements, her favorite.

Uncle Bob's service to the Advent followed his mother's devotion to the church. Among other support, she was founder of the Advent's endowment fund.

During my several terms as a church vestry member, a highlight of our luncheon meetings was Uncle Bob's attendance as senior warden emeritus.

XIV.
Country Gentleman

So where next for Robert Jemison, Jr., after he has developed much of Birmingham and neighboring cities?

Had I been a few years older (I was not yet a teen) and someone had told me he was becoming a farmer, I probably would have doubted that statement.

Not that there is anything wrong with farming. It was in the Jemisons' blood. Uncle Bob's ancestors had earned much of their livelihood from the soil in one way or another ever since the first Jemison set foot on American shores. But the man who had helped launch Fairfield, Ensley Highlands, Forest Park, Redmont and Mountain Brook, to name a few of his developments, now proposed planting crops, operating a dairy, and moving Aunt Virginia and their children out in the country?

That's not exactly what Uncle Bob had in mind.

As said, it's accurate to say that most Jemison families had been toiling in the soil to some extent, as had most early Americans; growing most or all the family's food was common practice, as were building a home and doing your repair work.

As I understand what Uncle Bob had in mind when he "moved to the country" in 1926, he wanted to become what was known then, and I suppose still is, as a country gentleman.

This handsome residence on Birmingham's northeastern outskirts was where Robert Jemison, Jr., moved his family so that he could begin life as a gentleman farmer. He succeeded in that venture as he had in others. (Courtesy, Weesie G. Smith)

He wanted to raise and ride horses. He wanted adequate space for Aunt Virginia to grow her flowers. He wanted to build and operate a dairy. And he eagerly anticipated the challenge of developing crops and orchards and improving farming methods in general.

Beyond those goals, Uncle Bob also wanted a place in the country for his grandchildren and other Jemisons to visit and enjoy.

Uncle Bob with his favorite horse at his country place. (Courtesy the Jefferson County Historical Society)

Mindful of his track record on land development, I can imagine how thoroughly he must have searched for the country place he wanted. He found it in northeast Jefferson County on Old Springville Road about 13 miles from downtown Birmingham.

Some background about the historic site is in order. In 1816, three years before Alabama became a state, early settlers built a log cabin there ultimately known as the Reed-

Riddle Home, thought to be the earliest dwelling in Jefferson County. Various additions and renovations changed the dwelling from pioneer to modern frame home with a wrap-around porch.

Uncle Bob decided the place was ideal for what would become his family's 500-acre Spring Lake Farms in 1926. Earlier he had consulted with Warren H. Manning, noted landscape architect from Boston, about plans for Mountain Brook. A Birmingham Historical Society newsletter reported that he and Manning, through correspondence and visits, discussed location of barns, orchards, entry and service drives, plus Aunt Virginia's personal gardens and the existing home to become his residence.

Behind the home was a special attraction, two lakes divided by a thin landstrip. A small cabin that once had housed a grist mill sat on the far side of one lake. The landstrip ultimately

The scenic lake that added charm to Spring Lake Farms.

vanished and the two lakes became one.

While there were two lakes, it was often said that the bottom of the smaller lake had never been found.

Only recently did I learn from Louise G. "Weesie" Smith, often referred to as the family historian, that the headwaters of Five Mile Creek, which runs through Jefferson County, are the lake water. The spillway always flows consistently, but I did not know until then where the water went.

To no family member's surprise, Uncle Bob's Spring Lake Farms soon were praised as a model farming operation comprised of a dairy with a herd of jersey cows, Arabian and Morgan horses, row crops, several orchards and magnificent flower and vegetable gardens.

Granddaughter "Weesie" Smith once observed that Uncle Bob ran the farms as an agricultural experiment station. He made clear that he hoped his research would benefit Southern agriculture.

National publications such as *Field Illustrated* described Spring Lake Farms as highly progressive. Uncle Bob had purchased the property in 1925; in 1946 he sold it to Emmet Ware and later it was subdivided as Spring Lake Estates.

In a nutshell, that is the serious side of Spring Lake Farms. There was a fun side, too. Not just for me, but for all the

Jemisons who visited there. And certainly for Uncle Bob's and Aunt Virginia's three children, and grandchildren who spent much family time there.

I was still a youngster when Uncle Bob bought and moved his family "to the country," as we thought of it then, and nothing pleased him more than to host Jemison family gatherings there. With his blessing, I also made adventurous bike trips there, along with Henry Badham, Van Scott, Bob Ramsay, Bob Shook and several others.

We were about 12 or 13 and having too much fun to get into devilment. We would oil up bike chains and check the air in our tires because there were no pumps beyond Roebuck. We would take goodies like vienna sausage, pork and beans, and cookies to eat along the way or after we got to the farm house.

My Airedale, Werp, trotted along with us a couple of times, and that added fun to the trip.

One route took us from Redmont to First Avenue North, through Avondale, Woodlawn, East Lake, Roebuck and Huffman. Sometimes we would alternate by turning east on Fourth Avenue South. Traffic was no problem because cars and streetcars were sparse. Soon after reaching Old Springville Road we arrived at Uncle Bob's and Aunt Virginia's farm home.

Uncle Bob would greet us, checking to see if we had enough

Service building and dairy farm at Spring Lake Farms. (Courtesy Weesie G. Smith)

goodies. If not, he would resupply us because he knew we would be "camping out" in the old grist mill; that was a really fun part of our visit.

Anyway he gave us the run of his place. We could check out the orchards and the neighborhood, have fun on the lake paddling around in a canoe, swimming, fishing, whatever. Then, bedding down on pallets, we would talk half the night and listen to sounds around the lake. Next morning we would check our farm surroundings again until time to bike back to Redmont.

Coming and going, I remember seeing lots of golfers at the Roebuck golf course. Later I would recall many of the regulars who played out there. And that Georgia's Bobby Jones won his first major tournament there, the Southern Amateur, in 1917.

Now when I pass the course I think of July 1951 when I played in an exhibition for the cancer fund drive with Ben Hogan, one of the greatest of all players. At that time the golf gallery was the largest-ever in Alabama. Hogan and I defeated Herschel Spears, assistant pro at the Country Club of Birmingham, and Paul Stapp, then a fine amateur player before turning professional.

Hopefully the City of Birmingham some day will restore Roebuck Golf Course to what it was in its glory days.

Uncle Bob sold his beloved Spring Lake Farms in 1948. I wondered then and now if the sale was necessary to generate cash to finish paying off his debts from the depression.

XV.
He Left Us a Better World

Having recalled the highlights of Robert Jemison, Jr.'s productive life from an admiring nephew's viewpoint, I now dare assessing his legacy. The assignment is daunting.

The closing words of the creed he adapted from orator Daniel Webster will not leave me: "...and see whether we, in our day and generation, may not perform something worthy to be remembered."

The foregoing pages reflect how well he performed. I am aware that my pride shines through, but shouldn't it? I believe it should.

I have felt for years that Uncle Bob's contributions to Birmingham, to Mountain Brook—perhaps my admiration overflows—to Jefferson County and by extension to Alabama and beyond—were well worth putting into print.

Thus, this effort, and again I express my thanks for assistance from individuals and institutions. I hope that what this remarkable, unselfish man did for his community and his fellow man is "something worthy to be remembered."

Appropriately, Uncle Bob's last home was this Mountain Brook residence on Balmoral Road. (Courtesy, Dave Mace and Birmingham Association of Realtors).

Aunt Virginia, Uncle Bob's beloved life partner, had died in 1953, but he apparently never anticipated retirement. As he neared his 90s, he was asked what contributed to his good health and long life. He responded, "Staying active in business and keeping an interest in the community and its continued growth."

He died with his boots on, appropriate for him his working boots. At age 96 he suffered a heart attack at his office and died that night, May 7, 1974.

He had requested that his funeral be brief and unpretentious, and it was. The Rev. C. Brinkley Morton conducted a simple service at the Church of the Advent. Burial was in Elmwood Cemetery.

Uncle Bob was not the retiring type. Here he is still at his desk in his 80s. (Courtesy The Birmingham News*)*

In a front-page story about Uncle Bob's passing, *The Birmingham News* commented, "For Birmingham it was as if the last great tree in what once had been a towering grove toppled and fell when Robert Jemison died Thursday night.

"At 96 he was the last of those first, almost legendary men of vision and just plain guts who made Birmingham—made it with their hands, their money, their sheer determination. They 'pulled this town up by its bootstraps,' Mr. Jemison had mused some 15 years ago, remembering on his 81st birthday those times when Birmingham was little more than a wide spot in the muddy road."

On its editorial page, the *Birmingham Post-Herald* observed: "To the very end he was a forward-looking man of vision, a lively, hearty individual who loved life and lived it with the rare combination of outstanding success and humility."

Because of his vision, so very many of us—past, present and future—owe him so much for what we enjoy today. As so many others said to him during his lifetime, "Thank you, Mr. Bob."

About the Authors

This Robert Jemison, Jr., biography is the second team writing effort for Elbert Jemison, Jr., of Mountain Brook and Wendell Givens of Birmingham. Their first, published in 1997, was *Playback: from Hickory Nuts to Hall of Fame*, a recounting of Jemison's amateur golf career and his military experience as a U.S. Army captain in Europe in World War Two for which he was awarded the Combat Infantryman Badge, two Bronze Stars, and medals for five major battles.

Jemison attended Sewanee Military Academy, the University of Virginia and the University of Alabama. He is married to the former Jess Ann Yarbrough of Huntsville. Their children are Anne Jemison Heppenstall, Elbert S. "Bo" Jemison, III, and Richard Rand Jemison. Grandchildren are Baker and Jess Heppenstall.

Primarily tutored by professional Sam Byrd, Jemison won back-to-back Alabama amateur golf championships and back-to-back state senior association championships. He was inducted into the Alabama Sports Hall of Fame in 1982.

A native of Lawrence County, Alabama, Givens attended Sidney Lanier High School in Montgomery and Howard College (now Samford University) in Birmingham. In a half-century newspaper career, he was on the *Alabama Journal* sports staff, the *Birmingham Age-Herald* sports staff and held editing positions with *The Birmingham News.*

Givens edited three sports books by the late Benny Marshall and wrote *Ninety-Nine Iron,* an account of the 1899 Sewanee (University of the South) football season during which Sewanee defeated five major-college opponents in only six days.

Givens and his wife, the former Mary Anne Boswell of Ensley, are parents of daughters Lynn Ray, Becky Freeman and Drew Willis. Grandchildren are David and Todd Ray, Tyler and Ashley Freeman, Katie and Jackson Willis.

Jemison

Givens